Ripples

Ripples
Hills Poets

Acknowledgements

Some of these poems have been published previously in various poetry publications.

Thanks

Thanks to Graham Catt for our cover photographs
(Mt Lofty Botanic Gardens)

Ripples
ISBN 978 1 76041 898 4
Copyright © text Hills Poets 2020
Cover photographs: Graham Catt

First published 2020 by
GINNINDERRA PRESS
PO Box 3461 Port Adelaide 5015
www.ginninderrapress.com.au

Contents

The Original Song	Belinda Broughton	9
Where a Tree Was	Belinda Broughton	10
Hair Fire Moon Tears	Belinda Broughton	11
Drawing Lesson From Kids	Belinda Broughton	12
Ode to a Lone Spider	Cary Hamlyn	13
Moment of Departure	Cary Hamlyn	14
Insomnia	Cary Hamlyn	15
She thought her voice was frail	Darrell Coggins	16
Gaps on the Wall	Darrell Coggins	17
Let Pass By	Darrell Coggins	18
Ridges in the sand	Darrell Coggins	19
Churchyard at Holy Cross	David Harris	20
I will not be cremated	David Harris	21
Faux Fur	David Harris	22
An Orison in Flame	David Harris	24
Jelly Mould	Elaine Barker	25
The Ansonia Clock	Elaine Barker	26
The Flycatcher	Elaine Barker	27
Glass	Elaine Barker	28
The Power of Two	Ian Coulls	29
La Belle Saison	Ian Coulls	30
The Hermit	Ian Coulls	31
Pablo Neruda and I	Ian Coulls	32
The Girls on the Factory Floor	Jill Gower	33
Moon Crystals	Jill Gower	34
Things I Like About Sunflowers	Jill Gower	35
Isadora Duncan's Last Dance	Jill Gower	36
Bay of Islands – Evening	Jules Koch	38
Windscape	Jules Koch	40
A CFS Officer Contemplates…	Jules Koch	41

Bird Calls in July	Karen Blaylock	42
Vignette	Karen Blaylock	43
Giving the Nod to Rain	Karen Blaylock	44
The Poetry of Leisure	Karen Blaylock	45
Better…? Or worse?	Louise Nicholas	46
Hypochondrium	Louise Nicholas	47
Wood sculpture	Louise Nicholas	48
Haiku	Maeve Archibald	49
Tanka	Maeve Archibald	50
One	Maeve Archibald	51
Funeral Music	Maeve Archibald	52
At Crafers Roundabout	Margaret Reichardt	53
Perhaps	Margaret Reichardt	54
On Beige	Margaret Reichardt	55
A Prayer	Margaret Reichardt	56
Cathedrals of the Wind	Michael Larkin	57
The Pendulum of Leather Rags	Michael Larkin	58
First Words	Michael Larkin	59
The Magpie	Michele Langman	60
Queen of Time	Michele Langman	61
Battleground	Ros Schulz	62
Golden Orb	Ros Schulz	63
Dinosaurs Don't Die	Ros Schulz	64
Port Adelaide 1945	Ros Schulz	65
Onkaparinga	Rosemary Winderlich	66
On signing petitions on Facebook	Rosemary Winderlich	67
Meadows to Echunga	Rosemary Winderlich	69
Dancing in the street	Rosemary Winderlich	70
If each day started out this way	Ruth Robinson	71
Unwelcome Companion	Ruth Robinson	72
Clouds from an aeroplane window	Ruth Robinson	73
Daybreak	Ruth Robinson	74

Winter vignette	Valerie Volk	75
Streuselkuchen	Valerie Volk	76
The moon in the morning	Valerie Volk	77
Night flight	Valerie Volk	78
Knitting Beanies	Zena Coote	80
It Wasn't a Special Day	Zena Coote	81
Bride of Christ	Zena Coote	82
Kangaroo Island Wilderness Trail	Zena Coote	83
The Authors		85

The Original Song

Such a small parcel of darkness to produce such light,
the clean, clear notes tumble all day, these days,
from his high twig.

He came into the world
with the song he sings, this blackbird.
Who knows what he feels?

We came bearing a song also,
but have forgotten it,
replaced it with a lament.

The lament is about suffering.
I expect to sing it all my life.
I expect to hear it from every voice.

In another room, my loved one
watches videos and cries.
Beauty makes him cry, as does kindness.

Well, we all cry about kindness as if it was unusual.
We cry about breaking through boundaries, overcoming trials,
We cry about hope. These are our laments.

But what if our essential song is a song of joy?
What if our song is as simple as the blackbird's?
And what if, suddenly, we all remember it

and sing?

Belinda Broughton

Where a Tree Was

There is the problem
of the sun
shining in
like vengeance
now
that the tree is gone.

Yesterday it stood in vivid life.
Today it's a pile
of firewood and chips.
And only because
we built our house
next to it.

Thirty years
living together
sharing the space
breathing
each other's breath
and now it's gone.

Yesterday I cried
into the huge space
where it isn't.
Today the sun
shines in
like vengeance.

Belinda Broughton

Hair Fire Moon Tears

What is the old man doing
with his hair on fire
while the moon weeps?

The moon's tears and his hair are one flow,
water and fire mirroring each other
through the thin veneer of the possible.

One flows up, one down.
One consumes, one nourishes.
But what is the old man doing?

Well, he's grieving of course,
having lost so much that his body
is almost in the earth.

So much seen and so much done
his own husk has grown too hard
for him to see the sprouting seed

despite the fire alight in his hair
and the moon, almost empty now
of tears.

Belinda Broughton

Drawing Lesson From Kids

Erratic all morning
running and squealing, loving and fighting,
the kids settle to drawing.

I join in with my tidy spirals
and neat leaf shapes.

They scrub the darkness into their paper,
unfold their stories, image by image.

Emboldened by these generous pencils,
he plunges into his night terror.
The night encroaches like a monster
right from the edges of the A4.

Spring willows weep onto her page
into blue water flowing around rocks,
foam bubbling.

This is the scene from which, earlier,
they brought buttercups in hot handfuls.

My drawing bores me so I ask for help
and they lean over casually
and scribble on my page.
It is immediately enlivened.

Now I can draw the yellow gloss of buttercups
down from the black vase
and onto paper.

Belinda Broughton

Ode to a Lone Spider

For months you hung in the corner
unmoving, still as a grave
each day a new meditation
a celebration of Nothingness
Maybe this is Nirvana?
Being without being
seeing but not feeling

Aeons passed before you moved
even then, we didn't witness it
as children play at 'Statues'
so you revelled in deception
pretending a life that's dead
or perhaps a death that's living

Daily we watched you
from the lavatory seat
little Lilliputian
strung in your web
oblivious to us
a careless foot, a stagger
would have fixed you

Then one day you erupted
gave birth to your spidery swarm
a hundred tiny, mindless things
scuttling over a desert of tiles
all looking to peg out a web
in a corner of their own

Cary Hamlyn

Moment of Departure

The sharp poignancy of airports
of arrivals and departures

data boards flashing with
international flights

time gained or lost
a moment of still-thereness

she turns
long red hair whips the air
gives one last wave

her smile hangs suspended
her image shimmers

then hovers in the cleft
between love and loss –

is gone

Cary Hamlyn

Insomnia

Fear nestles its head in the pillow
where sleep has become a stranger –
where worries clamour to be heard.

This cacophonous playground
of neuronal warriors are now
battling it out to kill off my sleep.

They have routed slumber from its present,
while the past shakes its maracas
at the future –
now a screeching violin.

Cary Hamlyn

She thought her voice was frail

Catapulted along
incidental on red dirt roads
she collects archival songs

And now in the belly of night –
tiptoeing past
an ordinary motel room

painted tea towels
memories on the wall

with the joy of uncertainty
dances on fragile glass

Clasped in a wraparound gown
crackling gentle against her skin
her repertoire undressed

Sweeping a palm across her face
ultimately alone

faintly sibilant –

from a blood-red mouth
she casts a lilt
to her past

Darrell Coggins

Gaps on the Wall

Crumbly on the seafront

a comfortably seedy hotel
last drinks long since called

thongs stuck to the floor –
in their usual places
for a while

a three-piece band plays
three chord songs to ghosts

Front door chocked open –

still chirpily bright
corners flapping

blown larksome across the bar

scrabbled into the cleft
of my hand –
a poster turns into a poem

phantom white as driftwood

gaps on the wall
accommodate where pictures were

Darrell Coggins

Let Pass By

Then…and then you drift past,
let pass by –
so soon a remnant shadow

numbed, leaning pensive,
elbow on the windowsill
I look away

Leftover tendrils –
patterns on the edge of calico curtains
shackle against my skin

both ornaments and handcuffs,
overlooked slender curls –
bracelets of light abate

A fist against my chin

a quickening shudder –
so soon night's cobwebs
will return

Withdrawn in that wounded room –
wristed, mute with apprehension
I unhook the rest of the day

Darrell Coggins

Ridges in the sand

Numb under a dawning sky
he drags heavy boots

Dwelling on small things
that go unnoticed
wisps of drawings
stacked in his suitcase

absent from himself –
he looks back
with mute superstition

Mapped with longing
postcards on the shelf
almost touch

lingering between each space
traced by soft fingertips

pencil-thin ridges in the sand

collapsing inwards
handwritten poems
closely held…

Darrell Coggins

Churchyard at Holy Cross

We look up, towards the west,
and doing so, look back in time.
Carefully marked plots dissolve
into grassy mounds.
Stones, tilt and lean,
words go from undecipherable
to barely discernible.
Disappear entirely after
400 years or so.

As the astronomer's telescope
displays events in the far-distant past,
so is this field a time capsule,
holding here the pages of history
of this tiny village.
Its ancient abbey still draws
worshippers – and tourists.

Behind us, towards the entrance gate
there lies a newer field of tiny plaques.
Not children's graves, but ashes,
each stone lies above
an urn, of last remains.

What will this be like in 400 years?
A necessity. So many people.
Ancestral links weaken and fade.
The passing of time is
so clearly marked in this
green field behind the church.

David Harris

I will not be cremated

It is foolish to lose joy of life while fearing death at all times...
for death is the nature, not the punishment of humankind.
Latin funerary inscription, 2nd–4th century CE

I will not deny my fellow creatures,
animal or plant
their use of this flesh,
built up from decades of consumption.
It is their turn now.
Every living thing must take its place
within a food chain,
consuming others during life,
feeding others after death.
Gone, for most of us,
the wolves, lions, bears,
rejuvenating humankind,
removing the slow, the old,
the sick, the unlucky.
Is there life after death?
Of course. We live on
as tiny creatures, plants, fungi.
Food for further levels in the chain.
When my life ends
it's me that ends, not life.
Now every molecule
of what I used to know as me
is now part of another form of life.
Tell me, is there a greater miracle?
Life itself is everlasting.
Death, simply a transition.

David Harris

Faux **Fur**

That *faux* fur stole looks good on you
so soft, so warm, so cuddly.
The winter wind just cuts right through
but you're enclosed and snugly.

Your friends all think it looks just great,
except for dearest Angie.
Her face afire and filled with hate,
she's very, very angry!

You said *faux fur*, it didn't help.
She said *for goodness sake –*
you're wearing FUR, her voice a yelp
how many faux'd that take?

And so she's forced me to rethink
my thoughts on man-made molecules.
With plastic fur replacing mink
and threads replacing follicles.

Deep in some dark, satanic mill
each baby *faux* is seen
cut from its mother's body, still
warm from the great machine.

Thrown into a plastic bin,
their fur entirely man-made,
a quivering pile of new *faux* in
a truck on road to rag trade.

But now you see that furry *faux*
comes not from trappers' toil,
it makes you feel quite good to know
it starts its life as oil.

David Harris

An Orison in Flame

We walked back through the church
hand in hand
then, at the door, looked back.

There were our two candles
young, upright, flames burning bright
in the glittering tray of votives

Most had burned down,
some halfway,
guttering flows of wax down their sides
flames flickering.

Others at their end of life,
short wicks supporting tiny flames
others now cold and lifeless

Each candle is an orison,
Prayed today, and signed with flame
saying, 'We were here – thinking of you.'

Our candles witness our presence here
and while they still burn, they
keep alive our witness.

David Harris

Jelly Mould

There's verve and a mellow warmth
in the copper that forms this jelly mould.
See how light catches each curve
of its fluted sides and again
at the base where a floral design shapes
the jelly that, with a plop, comes slithering out.

Consider Harriet the young kitchen hand.
Under Cook's direction she'll hold the mould
in hot water but only long enough
for the glistening shape to slip away
and, if she's lucky, it will sit
precisely in the centre of the crystal serving dish.

It would be her wish to taste the jelly
or at least to see it grace the banquet table,
but that handsome young waiter Emanuel
will carry it in. He'll put it down
and later take her arm and show her
the grandeur of the setting under candlelight.

Elaine Barker

The Ansonia Clock

Its place is on my kitchen shelf.
My clock directs my days, surveys me,
its ways unchanging.

A wooden fretwork forms a topknot
above a commanding face
where Roman numerals mark the hours.

Below, the pendulum, a silver disk,
swings steadily back and forth,
that sound unexceptional.

Best of all, the glass door carries
a catching design of bamboo fronds
and a tracery of flowers.

I've known my clock for over sixty years.
It relies on regular winding.
and even when I pass on the task

the steady beat will measure time long
after I am gone, that simple sound
the mainstay of a home.

Elaine Barker

The Flycatcher

Form follows function and reaching high
this glass dome is topped by a neat glass stopper.
At the base three sturdy feet lend stability.
You may wonder at the configuration:
the way the dome's base turns up, then in
to provide a continuous inner rim.
Here beer was placed to entice
blowflies and other insects to slip inside.
And so the teeming mass was trapped.
On a kitchen shelf or dining-room dresser
in every colonial house or homestead
the flycatcher admirably fulfilled its function.

Today a soapy wash, a rinse and polish
has given the piece its jaunty lustre.
Despite its humble past it has outlasted
other less sturdy glass.
My guests can never guess its use,
its age or worth. I let it stand
beside a copper jelly mould,
as a handsome curio on my side table.

Elaine Barker

Glass

'*A glass,*' she repeated with a smile
and as I waited for her to tell me
where to find that everyday object,
a thing of utility and mundane appeal,
I realised that the meaning of this common word
had absconded, had cut and run.
Standing in the kitchen she'd known
for over fifty years she'd lost her bearings,
had lost knowledge of words and meanings,
and the working days we'd shared.
Yes, some water was what she needed
but as time slipped by I stood there waiting.
I pointed to the yellow cupboards
but a wry grimace was her sole response.
So I found a glass, filled it at the tap
and she drank greedily and fast.
She took a deep breath
and retrieved the words '*thank you*'.
Then drawn to her past,
or still mindful of manners,
she thought to lift her right hand
and to wipe dry each side of her mouth.

Elaine Barker

The Power of Two

I struggle in these sunset hours
I would have spent with you.
The richness of life's treasure
is double shared by two
and better if we're lovers
the way it used to be
and better if you want to share
the rest of life with me.

And sometimes on the long, long haul
to the other side of night
we'd shelter from the world
till morning's early light.
Stereo is better,
life's richer to the power of two.
If ever there were paradise
I thought it there with you.

Ian Coulls

La Belle Saison

August fifteen
Day of the Assumption
Mary's rise to higher realms
to see to those below.

August fifteen
the day Jacques Prévert saw you
young and hungry pavement girl
hoping for a handout.

August fifteen
Place de la Concorde
the square of liberation
symbol of the future.

Did someone come
and give you bread
take you home
give you warmth
tell you it would be all right?

Did someone come
and give you love?

Did Mary come
and lift your load?

Ian Coulls

Published in *Words* (Ginninderra Press, 2017)

The Hermit

The hermit's gone
on holiday at home
and spends his time
waving to those outside.

Fondly suckling
delusions of grandeur
he sees the pilgrims pass.

But only I
who have climbed
his holy mountain
so many times
to find him
kissing the mirror,

I who have
scaled his holy mind
so many times
to find it fogbound,

only I can sit back,
with thumbs in belt
and say I do not know.

Ian Coulls

Published in *Words* (Ginninderra Press, 2017)

Pablo Neruda and I

'I want you to know one thing,'
Neruda wrote
and told a woman
his love was true
so long as she loved him.

I've never loved that way.
The loves I've known
have never died,
just the man I was
or the woman loved.

With the passage of time
we all change
and I can't regret
the passing of the man I was.

But each new love
has seen me grow,
grow to know
the man I am.

Each new love
has led to this,
this late, late bloom.

This last flourish
has led me now to you
and in my midnight hour
one burst of glory
like the final flare
from a sinking ship.

Ian Coulls

Published in *Danse Macabre* (Ginninderra Press, 2016)

The Girls on the Factory Floor

(Ford Motors, Dagenham, Essex, UK)

the girls on the factory floor
couldn't stand it any more.
they'd had enough of the summer heat
and working in their bras.

enough of the leaking roofs
and the gales in winter,
the rain dripping over them
from the corrugated iron

of the converted aircraft hangar.
enough of the pigeons
that sometimes dropped
down onto their tables

as they worked the assembly line,
sewing the heavy fabric for car seats.
they'd had enough of industrial machines
the needles that jabbed incessantly

as they tried to turn the fabric,
terrified of stitching their fingers.
now the girls on the factory floor
demanded equal rights and pay,

would not back down.
called a strike and won their case.
the girls on the factory floor
knew they would not be beaten again.

Jill Gower

Moon Crystals

(Haibun)

Rays of sunshine suffuse the room. Centre of table, a bunch of deep purple pansies. A silver dish, full to the brim with moon crystals, sits between the two women who face each other across the table. One with short dark hair whose name is Sara, the other with long hair, coiled on her neck, is called Bella. They look deep into each other's eyes. A tear is creeping down Bella's cheek.

Sara's slim hand pulls the dish of moon crystals closer to them both, then places her hand on top of Bella's hand and squeezes gently, compassionately.

Life has thrown some hurdles lately, and Bella has fallen hard. Sara lets go of Bella's hand, and sprinkles a few crystals into her open palm. They are symbols of hopes and dreams. Moon crystals, they say, help to calm and relieve stress.

Bella holds them in her hand; she is finding them mesmerising. She opens her fingers and lets them run through, watching as they fall like raindrops onto the table, gleaming in the sunlight. She thinks they are beautiful. Starts to smile as she looks up at Sara. Already, the pain is lifting from her eyes.

> moon crystals
> flow of life
> returning

Jill Gower

Things I Like About Sunflowers

brilliant yellow fluttery petals
the way they bring sunshine inside
when I put them in a vase

their nodding heads
reminding me of wise people
hobnobbing together

Van Gogh's sunflower paintings
and Tuscan fields full to the brim
with happy flowers

and I like their dark brown centres
like honeycombs, utopia for bees
buzzung happily in the hot sun

Jill Gower

Previously published in *Alchemy*, Friendly Street Poets 43, 2019

Isadora Duncan's Last Dance

(1877–1927)

Isadora
loved
to love
to live
to dance barefoot

Grecian tunics
scarves that drape or cling
changing dance forever

scandalous always
on stage in Boston
in her last American tour
she bared her breast
waved a red scarf
'this is red, so am I'

one blue-skied day
she went for a spin
with her friend Bugatti
and as they drove off
called out to friends
'I am off to love'

around her neck
a scarf
long and sheer
a silken rainbow
floating softly behind her

in Bugatti's car
the scarf caught
in an open-spoked wheel
tightened violently
around her neck

the tragedy
of her final dance

Jill Gower

Bay of Islands – Evening

1

at the edge of our sight
the day is closing

a lip smear
of burnt orange
above the horizon line

blends with a scoop of egg yolk
moments before setting

2

a scramble of shadows
as they merge with
one another

a slow release of gull wings
across the sky

as waves are filing their teeth
against rocks

and the tide is arm-wrestling
the shore

3

pressing against the bladder of a wave
the last surfer rides in

almost overstaying
his welcome

he quick-draws onto
the pebbled beach
with his reputation enhanced

4

the branches of the Norfolk pines
are fluttering
their false eyelashes
all the way along the coastal road

from a row of holiday cabins
a cigar puff
of smoke
escapes from a chimney

the first log of night

Jules Koch

Windscape

         a sudden
air-raid of wind

blows open the sky

clawing out sounds
from every object
it touches

along the avenue
the wind is lawless
amongst skirts
and over-familiar with hair

clouds have flocked to one
                  end
of the main street

while the high-rise buildings
hold their nerve

and a crane its cargo

Jules Koch

A CFS Officer Contemplates the Universe

after the longest
of bushfire seasons

the sunset still burns
a firebreak line

the night sky is a deep
dry well

stars are sparks
scattered across a
blackened landscape

nightly the moon
rebuilds itself

Jules Koch

Bird Calls in July

Top-knot pigeons on the cyclone fence
walking steadily along the bar
grey steel, grey pigeon, grey weathered posts;
there is such quietness in grey.

It is mid-July. Bird calls are clear
the sounds are peaceful and pure
the silences, in themselves, are full,
listening is Zen-like. The air is still.

Karen Blaylock

Vignette

Cockies sail on sunlit wings
across a swath of green
flying east against the sun
across the tranquil hills, in June.

Birds in the garden, fly low,
as swift as cockatoos are slow;
I'm looking for a word for peace,
there is only peace.

Karen Blaylock

Giving the Nod to Rain

(For Papa)

I remember just these skies at just this time
of year, gardening in and out of rain,
how you called the weather *showr'y,*
pronouncing it with care, never wishing
things to be other than they were.
It was patience filled the intervals,
enough for you and me. The clearings came
like miracles of light, and if it turned
to weather, we'd shelter and listen
to the dance on tin and you'd deliver
your amen, *gives 'em a good drink,*
was all you said, and made it sound
like something; you'd give a nod
and rock heel-toe and say the same again.

Karen Blaylock

The Poetry of Leisure

The canvas is the colour of brown paper
making us think of China, long ago,
the folds of her dress flow like a river

his inks are the colours of leaves of sage
lavender stems, shades of brown;
he paints, the poem of the age.

Leng Mei's long gone,
his *Ten Beauties*, gone
the deer beside her, in the garden, gone

yet here he is, Leng Mei,
his hand, his eye,
his courtesans

in the quiet,
in the muted light
as lovely, as the stillness,
in their way.

Karen Blaylock

Better…? Or worse?

Would that I could but I can't wear glasses.
The optometrist's spectacular skill
is no match for corneas that come to a point
where none is called for.
Better…? Or worse? He'd ask, as he slid
another lens into position and waited
while I considered relative clarity
where clarity increased in direct proportion
to the gradual distortion of the image.

Keratokonis, he announced.
and with no other clear course forward
prescribed contact lenses
that flatten as they focus
and deter distortion.

All praise the day the contact lens
fell from the mind of man and into the service
of eye-blighted, blind-sighted people like me…
And please God hold back the day
when the palsy plague my senior years
and a contact lens, poised on a fingertip,
and lifting inexorably to an eye,
is momentarily sent off-course by a sudden tremor,
and comes to rest in the drear and dingy darkness
of a nasal cavity.

Louise Nicholas

Hypochondrium

When I'd wallowed in sea and sky for fear of the dark,
when I'd chosen a spot for my commemorative plaque,
when I'd counted the blessings on my family tree,
and given thanks they'd outlive me,
when my 'something insidious'
had been downgraded to something the fastidious
amongst us would rather not mention –
and sitting required no buttock tension…

I woke to find bruises on cleavage and breasts
then resigned though I was to more doctors and tests,
to funeral plans and lamentation
found them to be, by taste and summation,
chocolate – best not eaten by insomniacs
who are also hypochondriacs.

Louise Nicholas

Wood sculpture

One day, he took a pocketknife
to an offcut of wood and fashioned a face:
ears, nose, a receding chin, an expression
fixed and pitiless as the Easter Island monoliths
that make a stand on a clifftop
and command the sea to come ashore.

For forty years, it stood
on my mother's mantelpiece,
for no other reason
than that her much-loved son made it.

And if now it stands on my mantelpiece,
as stubbornly lockjawed and monolithic
as when I pass him in the street,
it's for no other reason
than that my much-loved brother made it.

Louise Nicholas

Haiku

the scarecrow
kimono-clad
strikes a pose

on the hillside
a small temple
the overseer

the escarpment
a washing line
hung on the sky

Maeve Archibald

Tanka

my family
splinters of love
uncrushable
a strong woman
my mother Lillian

almost yesterday
the light lingers
on dry grass
the picnic basket
packed with memory

Maeve Archibald

One

One large Doberman frolics
One man with blond dreadlocks
One sail dodging the horizon
One lifeguard flexing pectorals
One bikini polka-dotted
One inflatable tube filled with children
One treasure seeker seeking
One child taking a walk alone
One ball bouncing high
One obese man ferrying water
One wave as high as the sky
One mother with one breast
A one-legged seagull
Takes it slow
Likewise, a woman
Also one-legged

Maeve Archibald

Funeral Music

the day of the funeral it rained
the sky was black and sombre
matching the mood
of the mourners
gathered from
the far reaches
of friendship
and close memory
near to the heart

the sky wept
and so did we

Maeve Archibald

At Crafers Roundabout

I thought it was a weed at first,
a green sprout on the roadside,
forcing its way through grey concrete,
finally it bloomed,
a scarlet poppy.
As I passed daily, I eagerly looked for it,
alas when it died,
no more buds came,
I hope the seeds found a better place to live
rather than that blasted kerb.

Margaret Reichardt

Perhaps

Don't you wish
men could invent something
that didn't have an aftermath,
not killing trees or animals,
or fogging the air.
Someday, the purple people will say
what an interesting planet,
it was habitable once,
wonder what happened there?

Margaret Reichardt

On Beige

Why is she wearing a beige dress?
It's the colour of skin
and tones with her hair
really, if she turned her face away
she wouldn't be there
a no-colour that gives nothing
so either her wish is to disappear
or her vibrant mood is to conquer all –
overpower us with the personality of her smile.
Perhaps she should be wearing red.

Margaret Reichardt

A Prayer

I think we should pray for poets
those poor unfortunates
lost in a forest of phrases
or adrift on a sea, empty of ideas
May sunlight shimmering on gum leaves
or a koala sedately rocking
in a wind tossed tree
give them good thoughts
or may the total stillness
of a hot summer's day
send them scrambling for notebooks
to hold these fragile webs of words
unless, like a leaping kangaroo
the words vanish from sight
into the scrub, forever.

Margaret Reichardt

Cathedrals of the Wind

I drank the milk of fire
in the cradle of the mountains

Listened to the rain
in the classroom of the trees

I raised cathedrals of the wind
in the slavery of the grasslands

Searched for gods, washed ashore
in the graveyard of the sea

Michael Larkin

The Pendulum of Leather Rags

The mass of morning has begun,
chrome altars steam and hiss, as the city wakes
from troubled dreams, winter drags its bones.

Disciples press the narrow lanes
in the pendulum of leather rags,
jostling for an empty chair, a place to call their own.

Fingers frayed like old rope
strive to thread the well-dressed lines,
that dust across the tables, between designer smiles.

Skinned pears with pearls of cream
masquerade their weary ways, holding high
an image, they no longer comprehend.

Sculptured ice enthrals their mirrors,
captures fleeting charm, to grace the world
with button love, praise of unknown friends.

Day by day, pay by pay, furrows deepen
on the brow, looking down upon their circles
of flat white euphoria.

Michael Larkin

First Words

Beneath the state of censored dreams
Immortal wires and armoured drones

Tunnels of unending canvas
Dark flowers of the fortress world

Beauty held in desecration
Labyrinths of art unseen

Beyond the bounds of common lives
Confessions of their covered crimes

Without a face, without name
I bare myself upon the walls

Ghost my first words
In the light of broken moons

Michael Larkin

The Magpie

The poet notates the silence in the dark
Too early woken by a magpie
Dropping jewels into that silence.
His delicate melisma a thread of honey
Flung out in curlicue whorls
Across the pool of darkness
Carelessly, for he has more.
Sings again his silver flute, and pauses,
'Beat that, yokels!
I am the Mozart of magpies.
I am your Queen of the night.'
He knows I am listening though I am not his bird
He feels my ear is on him, that I've forgone annoyance
For bliss.

The poet chronicles the dawn
Maps the blossoming of light
Increments of colour
Brightening into day.

Michele Langman

Queen of Time

The clock it ticking and thus am I rich
For I am Queen of Time commanding hours
To myself.
Here is my wealth, my bag full of time
Golden with old clocks
Their delicate mechanisms counting silver minutes
Into my bags of Time. Thus am I rich
With space to move unhurried
Through entire days, sorting memories as they arise
Savouring old songs
Counting my treasures.
Time is my wealth for I know how to spend it
And thus am I rich.

Michele Langman

Battleground

Sharing a fridge teaches you the yin
and the yang of it, not necessarily leading
to harmony in the arctic universe.

Try to balance the contents the best way –
yours of course – and the atom splits.
You jostle for space like the stuff, find the dairy
down amongst the onions, contaminated
meat-in-waiting drips juice on cheese,
seldom-used pickles and pastes obstruct,
popular salads and snacks squeezed to the back.

Your hands buzz around shelves
like a fork-lift in a warehouse
locating allocating rearranging condensing
endlessly – this finite space is crammed
like my finite patience, by repetition.
Three separate bowls of lemon halves
tomato tops sprout everywhere
and never a whole tomato.

Round argues with square
flat things on the high shelf
leave tall soup galleons tilting
recklessly, nowhere to go.
Items elbow each other out of the way
like we do, set us establishing
our parameters all over again.

Ros Schulz

Golden Orb

How brazen of you to occupy that prime space.
Shadow puppet strung up against a grey white sky
between towering gutters and palm tree
tethered to a grassy stalk, like a guest at an art show
seated in the High Chair, showcasing your power
to your hapless catch trapped in your web –
the line getting longer and longer each day.
You provoke the wind that teases, like distant rumbles
of thunderstorm withholding rain like a secret.

Ah Nephilim, giant offspring of mysterious origin
your golden silk garnered for fishing nets, prized in
wedding garments, source of steely strength
in Astro Industry and Medicine – do you gloat
as your fine legs fold over and round your victim
while insects caught in the wings watch their destiny?

I brushed against your template –
that caused a frantic scrabble of legs
a stiff pose and then resume the task.
Was that contempt or a dare or resignation,
a humble playing out of your life?
It only needs a human to brashly tangle
and slash to shreds with arms and sticks
but in the morning, undaunted,
you will repair and spin again.

Ros Schulz

Previously published in *The Mozzie*, January/February 2014

Dinosaurs Don't Die

(after an exhibition of sand sculptures at Port Adelaide)

Stegosaurus' sharp scales challenge the skies
Pterodactyl severs the air with a wingspan of ten metres
Tyrannosaurus' eyes bulge with anger –
sculptures in red sand – each as big as a room
firm and grainy tail and spine
cut in geometric design –
we squint in awe in the summer glare.

The children are unfazed. Amy at three
keeps looking for the baby ones
sculpted cutely into the mother's hind leg,
Dan is wrestling with a loose fence post
and Sam is looking for something to climb
in the spiralling tracks and distorted trees.
In the workshop later, they mould and scrunch
tease up their brittle wet sand replicas.

Their dinosaurs are within
behind a lens we cannot probe,
fears and challenges we can't meet,
perhaps more lasting than these towering shapes
transient to time and wind,
already beginning to crumble.

Ros Schulz

Port Adelaide 1945

What did I know of the Black Diamond Corner
at four years old – let loose along the wharf
with older brothers, not to scavenge hunks of coal
fallen from the shipping – diamonds to the poor
but bent on adventure. Mum was terrified –
she had the baby to mind plus worked
in the cafe we lived above and my younger brother
rolled billycans down the bull-nosed balcony
onto streetwalkers below while my mother laughed
with the Yankee sailors, served them when they
swarmed in for a good meal.
I hid under the tables shyly (they enticed me out
with long sticks of gum) she never got over
the romance of the forces, so handsome in those uniforms
the local boys couldn't compete; she had
a brother in the air force too and I had
the best uniforms all through school
but never a shilling for a real dress.
For a treat they took us kids on their boat
the *Don J Carlos* gave us chewy gum and sweets.
We hugged the bollards, jumped along the gangplank
dangled our legs over the edge of the wharf
peered into the black oily water below till
mum couldn't stand it any more – we left pretty soon
for the safety of the country.

Ros Schulz

Previously published in *The Heart of Port Adelaide* (Ginninderra Press)

Onkaparinga

Four days driving…
late at night truck rolls to a stop
We five older ones
seated between truck cab and piano
stand sleepily…look over the top
headlights beam on gateway to new life
ghost gums glowing, river flowing
into our lives.

We…from brown water country
Muddy creeks, dams often dry
Here, singing water over stones glowing
sang into our lives.

Years of discovery, following the river
exploring each bend, each secret pool
engineering, creating dams
sluices, channels, diversions, designs…
Onkaparinga, through lush fields winding
flowed through our days.

Friendly, gentle in summer
welcome refuge from heat
in flood fierce and powerful
a different beat…
music of seasons
woven in to the fabric of our days.

Wherever I've travelled since then
Onkaparinga…clear and cool
lies sweet in my mind
part of my dreaming.

Rosemary Winderlich

On signing petitions on Facebook

Each one of us is only one
but if we hope, pray, scream for action
if our hearts are despairing, crying
for children mutilated, dying
families fractured, bodies distorted…
and those seeming beautiful and whole
with deep wounds, jagged scars in their soul
we will sign.
Perhaps you laugh at me
I know some cringe at my naivety
still I will stand and speak and post
and I will sign.

If we all discount the worth
of one voice, yours or mine
how can we expect change
on this poor, struggling earth
encrusted with corruption and shame?
If we each cringe in fear of ridicule
of looking too political
who will speak for the suffering?
If I withhold my voice, and you
who will speak for the dispossessed?
so add your voice to mine
and your presence…stand and say
there is a much better way.

If we are brave, and sign
stand, act together, we can be
a dam to stop the tainted wave.
Add your small light to mine…
soon more and more will shine
so the imprisoned, the refugee can see
they are not alone in their dark night
…and so I will sign.

Rosemary Winderlich

Meadows to Echunga

Timeless tunnel of trees
embracing the road…and me
strength and familiarity
…lush winter green grasses
cattle deep in rich pastures.
Dry white tufts of last year's grass
randomly scattered
pleasing my eyes, and I wonder why…
why do they speak sweetly to me
…imprint on childhood memory?
or is that they dilute the green
…rather overpowering?

I dream on through Meadows country
little towns lying gentle on my mind
lane names, memorials to pioneer families
recall faces of classmates at high school
bussing in from Macclesfield, Meadows.

Past Mylor my spirits damp down
Aldgate…last friendly little town.
Goodbye for a while to meanderings
soothed by childhood memories
nostalgia by the Onkaparinga
feast of sturdy, friendly gums
swaths of vigorous winter green
accented by white-tufted grass
that caresses my eyes…
I don't know why.

Back to the Freeway…too rapidly down
to a different country, Adelaide town.

Rosemary Winderlich

Dancing in the street

Sorry…but not really
sorry if you are embarrassed
children, grandchildren, friends
but I must listen to heart music
and sing…and dream…
and dance.

This gift I tried to give to you
rich heart store of music
welling up, overflowing…
looking over mountains, plains
drowning in your children's eyes…
music to paint pictures
build dreams.

Please
listen to the music in your hearts
dance with it if you can
let the songs flow through.
Sing to sky, hills, streams
and dream.

I will rejoice
to know you have this treasure
music in your heart
and dreams.

Rosemary Winderlich

If each day started out this way

If each day started out this way
How perfect it would be
The warmth of sun upon freed skin
The sky as blue as sea

Birdsong is the only sound
That fills the early hours
As through the hills I take my walk
Springs cherry trees in flower

The rows of trees that now awake
Shrug of their winter blues
They dress themselves for passers-by
In clothes of soft green hues

The railway line is silent
I run across the track
The scent of spring surrounds me
Morning sunshine on my back

Along the creek, back up the hill
Past Forest Lodge I roam
A skip within my footsteps
As I turn to head for home

Renewed by springtime's treasures
Her hills bounty shared with me
If each day started out this way
How perfect it would be

Ruth Robinson

Unwelcome Companion

A wolf tending the lambs of god
Disguised in cardinal red
Hiding behind papal robes
And holy walls

The blessed Mary's halo
Now a bright spotlight
Piercing the darkest corners
Of ingrained evil and buried sin

His twisted tongue
That has held dialect with the devil
Recoils as untruths fall
That a thousand Hail Marys could not forgive

An injured lamb bleats from the flock
Tells of his 'unwelcome companion'
Innocence, never feeling safe
Living in the shadows of self-harm
Carrying a heavy cross no child should ever bear

Tears well for all the lambs that have been led to slaughter
The hypocrisy of the cloth
If there is a god
Then the skeletons in his papal closet
Will stand sentry as he climbs the stairs to meet his maker

Ruth Robinson

Clouds from an aeroplane window

They float below me
Marshmallow mountains
Cotton wool, kapok
The inside of a doona bursting free
Eggwhite meringues
An endless sea of white foam
White fairy floss
Bubbles bursting forth from the washing machine

Yet should we fall they won't soften the blow

Now as we dip through the stratosphere
Towering icebergs
Bobbing on a cold grey sea
Smoke billows
Mist on the moors
Glancing sideways
An infinite distant arctic landscape
Devoid of life

A desolate place to end one's days

Looking down I can see
Black shadows cast on a patchwork landscape
Ink spots on a page
Moving far more slowly than the white herd above
Journeying above my head
A stampede of albino animals
Rushing through an endless blue tundra
Never reaching their destination

Back on the ground, looking up, I see clouds.

Ruth Robinson

Daybreak

Early morning slinks over the horizon
Silently creeping
Black silk rolled away
To reveal kaleidoscopic colour
A new day unfolds
Heralded by the sounds of early morning birdsong
The day's first broadcast
Morning's roll call, answered in unison
Dewpoint glistens, picked out by the first beams of light
Black trees stand in negative against a flame pink dawn

Ruth Robinson

Winter vignette

Small town in Germany.
A winter afternoon.
A chocolate shop
where tidy showcases
of tantalising treats
(Teutonic order!)
offer such temptation.
Irresistible!
Air fragrant with the smells
of coffee mingling with the chocolate.
Outside an icy chill.
But here inside
is warmth and happy company.
A culminating touch,
to watch through glass
the darkening streets
where first fine feather flakes of snow
come drifting down.

Valerie Volk

Streuselkuchen

Farm women, busy, focused,
in oven-heated kitchens,
rooms fragrant with the smells
of yeast and baking bread.
Great slabs of German cake,
the *streuselkuchen*, recipe
passed down through generations.
My grandmother, her daughters,
aproned, hair scragged back,
for this is serious:
the weekly baking day.

Today I stand, my kitchen
gleaming white with stainless steel,
and ponder on my forebears.
All those women, long since
crumbling into dust, while I,
as they once did, stir, sift and beat,
age-yellowed recipes at hand,
wondering if one day
the daughter I have taught these skills
will stir and sift and beat this cake,
and think of me with fondness.

Valerie Volk

The moon in the morning

Peach-coloured,
improbable balloon,
hanging suspended
in the lightening sky.
That moon,
a stately dowager,
sailing unperturbed
towards horizons
that beckon her to bed.
Beside her,
floating idly,
a rose wisp of cloud.
An acolyte
attends the progress
of the fading moon.

Valerie Volk

Night flight

Tense music.
Thickening shadows on the screen.
A stifled cry –
footsteps near
a cowering figure in the corner…
Plane movies.

Around me constant blanket noise
of throbbing engines
as we are borne high over unseen seas
thirty thousand feet below.
Outside, black night.
Within our confined safety,
stray pools of light show those
who, wakeful, envy sleepers
their fitful doze, twisting,
trying to accommodate distorting seats.
Somewhere a child cries restlessly
before subsiding once again.

Oh blessed sleep. Before my aching eyes
a woman's face, contorted, looms.
Then, hands clenched, she confronts
the spectral figure. A soundless scream.
Beside me, each side, sleepers twitch uneasily.
In this warm darkness, six hours passed
with eight to go, I sigh in envy.
Midnight's dinner still weighs heavily.
I contemplate the crisis on the screen.

Might as well replace the headphones
discover what the outcome was…
But no, the credits roll.
I'll never know.

Valerie Volk

Knitting Beanies

She sat in the wicker chair
Just like her mother had
Clicking away the hours
Creating, quietly industrious

The cushion low to her back
The crocheted rug
Softening the old woods
Enveloping her in comfort

Family around
Life taking its natural course
Fire crackling
Casserole on the hearth

And there she sat, clicking, clicking
Soon there was silence
The clicking was no longer
Her body giving way
To the pleasure of 'just being'

Small nasal breaths
Releasing the satisfaction of
Family life and the invitation
To stay and knit
Just one more beanie

Zena Coote

It Wasn't a Special Day

It wasn't a special day
A morning walk in the cemetery
The old arthritic legs of my companion
Galloping with expectation, of what I am not sure

Stones broken, illegible inscriptions and etchings
Their thoughtful words lost to the rigours of the weather
Broken vases of 'MOTHER' and 'FATHER'
Matching the sons and daughters, grandparents and babies

A small plane, on a small mound
'Fly high, little man…'
Fresh flowers, fresh tears
Love and sorrow palpable
For a short life, no longer in flight

So many people
So many lives
So many things unsaid
So many unhealed wounds

And yet, the silk flowers continue to smile
The sun will rise in the morning
Giving energy for me and my companion
To quietly walk the cemetery again tomorrow

Zena Coote

Bride of Christ

I was a good child
Socks pulled up high
Plaits arranged neatly on my head
A compliant, easy student

Asking for forgiveness
For lies not told
Biscuits not stolen
Rosary beads and kissing the crucifix

Lighting small thin candles for the poor
Purchased from pocket money
Praying in wooden rows
For salvation and deliverance from sin

Education based on fear and approval
Shining the brightest
Standing the straightest
I was a convent child

Picking the primroses for the elderly
Sunday church attended
All the family regimented and behaved
Irish, Catholic family

Student of the nuns
Was I good enough?
Was I clever enough?
Worthy enough?

Hail Mary, Mother of God
Where were you when I needed you?
I was only eight years old

Zena Coote

Kangaroo Island Wilderness Trail

Sheer cliffs
Sea spray in the face
Walkways seeking passage to the ocean
Picking our footsteps along rocky clifftops

Coastal winds
Ocean gardens of minuscule,
Dense bonsai clusters
Harbouring in eroded rock pools

White sands in timeless motion
Hooded plovers breed in reclaimed dunes
Away from our footsteps on the beach
Trail disappearing

Dense eucalyptus woodlands
Historic land clearing
Bordered by lagoons
Diverse habitats and pouched residents

Shaded gullies of bracken
Fallen trees, leaf litter carpet
Delicate orchids
Seen only in stillness

Nocturnal serenade of the boobook owl
Morning welcome of blue wrens and scarlet robins
Feeding on budding spikes of white flowering bottlebrush

Snakes bask motionless
Echidna quicken their scurry in the litter
A single koala stills for photos

We exit to our other world

Zena Coote

The Authors

Maeve Archibald grew up in NSW on a sheep farm. This early association with nature has been a lifelong inspiration in her life and poetry. She has been living in Adelaide with her family since 1990. Maeve's poetry has been published in the annual Friendly Street anthologies, and the two Hills Poets' anthologies.

Elaine Barker has been writing poetry for over three decades and her work has been published overseas and widely around Australia. In 2019, Ginninderra Press published her fourth collection *See My Feathered Fingers*, which highlights the small, commonplace articles that play such an important part in our lives and memories.

Karen Blaylock writes poetry and essays. She lives and works in the Adelaide Hills. Her book of poems is due to be published in 2020.

Belinda Broughton has practised as a visual artist all of her adult life and has been seriously engaged in poetry since 2004. She has three volumes of poetry published and has poems in national and international journals and anthologies. She is not keen on politicians but rather likes garden worms.

Darrell Coggins is a poet, visual artist and musician. His poetry has been published in *Poetry Matters*, *Positive Words*, *The Mozzie*, *Tamba*, *Studio*, *Nine Muses*, *Envy – Seven Deadly Sins*, *The Crow* and Friendly Street Poets anthologies. Darrell's poems are of moments seen, heard and felt.

Zena Coote, while still in a 'serious' working life, entered the world of words, expression, provocation, fun and observation, six years ago. It is called poetry and she says she loves it.

Ian Coulls has published three chapbooks of poetry, three books of short stories, and another book of poetry early in 2020. He has been published regularly in *The Australia Times* and anthologies by Ginninderra Press, Kensington Norwood Writers' Group, Friendly Street Poets, and the Tea Tree Gully Poetry Festival.

Jill Gower lives in the beautiful Adelaide Hills and is the convenor of Hills Poets. She has published four collections of poetry and has edited their first two anthologies, *Frost & Fire* and *Through the Tunnel*. Her work has been published in various anthologies and journals. She enjoys spending time with family and friends.

Cary Hamlyn is an Adelaide poet who has worked as a documentary film editor in Sydney and a social worker in Adelaide. She is the author of two chapbooks – *Scraping the Night* (Ginninderra Press, 2016) and *Ultrasound in B-Flat*) (Garron Press, 2017). She won the Satura Prize in 2017.

David Harris is a retired engineer. First poem in school magazine (1954). Occasional poems and song lyrics over the years. First publication, *In a Subjunctive Mood*, 2017. Second (chapbook) now with publisher. Also spends time playing Celtic/folk music (flute).

Jules Leigh Koch is an Adelaide poet and the author of five poetry collections. He has been a recipient of two South Australian Literature grants in 2008 and 2011 and of many awards. He was a guest reader at Adelaide Writers' Festival in March 2017 and a judge for the John Bray Festival Awards in 2017 and 2019.

Michele Langman lives in Mt Barker, was a drama and English teacher for many years and has written for most of her life. She wrote and performed her one-woman play *The Wishing Well* in the Festival Fringe (1992). In 2007 she published her book *Drama, Myth and Psyche*.

Michael Larkin is an emerging poet from Hahndorf in the Adelaide Hills/Peramangk Country. He is a life member of the Hahndorf Football Club and recent member of Hills Poets. Michael is a Kokatha man who works in the field of sexual health and blood-borne viruses.

Louise Nicholas has been a long-term member of the Adelaide poetry community. Her publications include *The Smear Test* and *The Mammogram* (both self-published); *WomanSpeak*, co-written with Jude Aquilina (Wakefield Press); *Large* (Garron Press); *The List of Last Remaining* (Five Islands Press); and *Meet My Mother* (Ginninderra Press).

Margaret Reichardt was born in Melbourne in 1943 and raised in country Victoria. She moved to the Adelaide Hills in the late 70s and never looked back. Margaret started to write poetry at the age of eleven and hasn't stopped yet.

Ruth Robinson is UK born and bred. Transported to Australia in the 70s, her childhood suitcase packed with a passion for books and the written word. Sharing words with fellow enthusiasts nourishes her, like sharing a beautiful meal nourishes others. To combine them both is perfection.

Ros Schulz has been represented in SA Friendly Street Poets anthologies since 1997, and in other local and interstate journals. Her first single collection of poems, *Weight of Evidence*, was published in 2010 by Ginninderra Press, and two chapbooks since. She co-edited *Friendly Street Poets Anthology No. 42* in 2018.

Valerie Volk is an award-winning Adelaide writer of poetry, verse novels, short stories and longer fiction. She is fascinated by the perennial question 'What if…?' and is a self-confessed voyeur of other people's lives. She loves film, travel, opera and cats – not necessarily in that order – but, most of all, she loves to write.

Rosemary Winderlich is a farmer's daughter, was a teacher who married a pastor and had six children. After her husband died, she was a prison chaplain and taught English. She loves the open road, the wind and the sea and is an explorer, a reader and a compulsive student, technologically challenged, not ageing gracefully.

www.ingramcontent.com/pod-product-compliance
Lightning Source LLC
Chambersburg PA
CBHW062142100526
44589CB00014B/1659